IN THE NEXT GALAXY

Ruth Stone

In the Next Galaxy

COPPER CANYON PRESS

The author expresses her appreciation to the editors of the
following publications, in which some of these poems first
appeared: *American Literary Review, American Poetry Review,
Feminist Studies, Green Mountain Review, Iowa Review, Massa-
chussetts Review, Mudfish, Paintbrush, Paterson Review, Texas
Review,* and *Vermont Magazine.*

Cover art: *Pear and Coconut,* oil on masonite by Olga Antonova,
courtesy of Tepper Takayama Fine Arts.

Copper Canyon Press is in residence under the auspices of
the Centrum Foundation at Fort Worden State Park in Port
Townsend, Washington. Centrum sponsors artist residencies,
education workshops for Washington State students and teachers,
Blues, Jazz, and Fiddletunes Festivals, classical music perfor-
mances, and The Port Townsend Writers' Conference.

LIBRARY OF CONGRESS CATALOGING-IN-PUBLICATION DATA

Stone, Ruth

In the next galaxy / Ruth Stone.

   p. cm.

ISBN 1-55659-207-8

1. Title.

PS3537.T6817 I54 2002

811'.54 — DC21   2001007424

COPPER CANYON PRESS

Post Office Box 271

Port Townsend, Washington 98368

www.coppercanyonpress.org

Abigail Stone's meticulous corrections and patient reading of multiple proofs were essential to this volume. During my recent loss of vision she has provided the light.

Contents

IN THE NEXT GALAXY

The Professor Cries

This is the end of March.
The tax collector
wants me to cut my wrists.
The roach inspector
drives up in a truck.
The snow sits like dough
turning sour. Every hour
love's bones grow lighter.
This is what comes
of having no pity.
Time used me.
Death used me.
I live in Johnson City.

Spring Beauties

The abandoned campus,
empty brick buildings and early June
when you came to visit me;
crossing the states midway,
the straggled belts of little roads;
hitchhiking with your portable typewriter.
The campus, an academy of trees,
under which some hand, the wind's I guess,
had scattered the pale light
of thousands of spring beauties,
petals stained with pink veins;
secret, blooming for themselves.
We sat among them.
Your long fingers, thin body,
and long bones of improbable genius;
some scattered gene as Kafka must have had.
Your deep voice, this passing dust of miracles.
That simple that was myself, half conscious,
as though each moment was a page
where words appeared; the bent hammer of the type
struck against the moving ribbon.
The light air, the restless leaves;
the ripple of time warped by our longing.
There, as if we were painted
by some unknown impressionist.

Always Your Shadow

When I remember the cold mornings
when we slept on your side of the sagging bed;
when I remember the cold edge of the curtain
where the light lay still as the marble edge
of the table where the phone wept, the last ring
in another country; that street of cold frost
and row houses, the gas lamps' pulsing light,
hesitant as your last heartbeats when you hung
by a silk cord on the back of a rented door.
This I often rearrange, I don't accept.
But you lived longer than Frédéric Chopin.
And your ancestors could have come from Warsaw.
Back then, I say, you could have died easily as he,
all those frail geniuses died of syphilis or TB.
In this cluttered room, I am listening to Chopin.
When the hurricane presses the ocean,
and the waters divide like the Red Sea,
though split in half, though split again and again,
what is retrieved is cast and taken as an offering.
As this formless slough that breaks apart,
that adheres and breaks, as the rubble of words,
as the metamorphosis of breath.

Looking at Your Hand

This shadow passing over your hand,
its bones like peacock's claws,
yellow waxed scales through diffuse colors.
Along the road's edge pale amberish grass,
each flexible high stalk capped with a seed pod.
Stored in unknown places in the skull,
confetti; temporal torn bits of the fractured whole.
Like flocks of small dark birds,
hidden parts of the self weep at these narrow
places of salt marshes crowded along
honeycombs of steel and plastic.
It will not resolve itself, the mystery of building blocks,
the runaway brutal, the power of nothing to multiply.
Turning the hand over to become the palm,
for a moment it can shape itself into a cup of water.

Seed

Corn is universal,
so like a Roman senator.
Its truths are silk tassels.
True its ears are sometimes
rotten, impure.
But it aspires in vast acres,
rectangular spaces,
to conspire with every pollinator
and to bear for the future
in its yellow hair.

And what are your aspirations,
oh my dears,
who will wear into tatters
like the dry sheaves
left standing, stuttering
in November's wind;
my Indian corn, my maize,
my seeds for a ruined world.
Oh my daughters.

In the Next Galaxy

Things will be different.
No one will lose their sight,
their hearing, their gallbladder.
It will be all Catskills with brand-
new wraparound verandas.
The idea of Hitler will not
have vibrated yet.
While back here,
they are still cleaning out
pockets of wrinkled
Nazis hiding in Argentina.
But in the next galaxy,
certain planets will have true
blue skies and drinking water.

Metaphors of the Tree

The play yard with its automobile tire
hanging from the one tree, like a lynching.

The tree wrapped around itself in multiple muscles;
a clump of trees come together under the bark,
twisting up; a corporate tree, the only tree in the yard.

The tree with its thousand subsidiaries
cluster-blooming, testing the air, expanding;
its product underground, growing chemicals;
pulling the guts from the soil, involved with the fungus.

The tree, tilting its leaves to capture bullets of light; inhaling,
exhaling; its many thousand stomata breathing, creating the air.

Then the absent tree when the play yard is paved with asphalt;
a blank space where the tree was, a space that the birds pass over,
where the wind does not pause.

Rising

In the government offices the rules and regulations
regarding erosion of beaches move from one file to another.
The sand whispers back into the undertow.
At the South Pole, part of the frozen continent splits
and melts, eating into the ice pack.
Along the Eastern Seaboard a house on the ocean
is lifted on stilts. It walks into the water.
The piles driven deep into the sand are at last exposed,
their thin bones fragile as tiny starfish.
The windows, blank eyes of dead seagulls,
catch the phosphorescence in the choppy waves.
The waves are as even as furrows in a cornfield.
But the house is moving in the opposite direction.
How mild the evening is. No one would suppose
that the house is going out with the tide.

Returning to the City of Your Childhood

In the framed black-and-white photograph
on the wall of your rented furnished condominium,
you imagine a hidden garden of blue cornflowers.
It drifts in the acid residue. In this black-and-white
photograph, the garden you imagine is beyond
a narrow passageway between two buildings.
For you, it exists in spite of this jerry-built
investment condominium. And you imagine
someone, perhaps it is you, in the hidden part
of the photograph; you, a child, are looking over
a plank fence to where surely, (you imagine),
a grandfather is nailing together piece by careful
piece an original wooden dollhouse
(not yours, it was never yours). In reality you once
watched him, that grandfather beyond the fence,
with your own trust in miracles, at age six.
In the room where the photograph (not yours) hangs,
a montage sharp as the odor of fresh sawdust.
You put your hand against the striated silence.
What are these things that draw toward us,
these visitors who hide among us,
who are as the air that enters,
giving and taking away...

Leaving My Roommates in New York

Snow falls upon snow fastening its delicate hooks.
As far as you can see in the Ukraine, snow.
In some places permafrost, as in that recent historic time,
mammoths were revealed in the great ice.
Sometimes birds freeze in the air and fall.
But from all that Yasha has escaped.
Here he is in New York
in the back room of Ivan's apartment;
although it is still in his head.
Even the young girl to whom
he teaches chess. She is only sixteen, so her mother
comes along.
Even they, when they go out in the evening,
feel the magnetic pull.
And Ivan, with four stepmothers
and assorted half siblings, Ivan with the lease,
sub-subletting his closet rooms with windows on brick walls,
his rentees living on the third floor
like Mongols in their yurts. He bargains among them
behind closed doors like a shadchan. Without Ivan,
they are on the street. But at this moment
I am going up to the spring ice; to the mountain,
to the empty farmhouse, to frozen floors,
to the subliminal sounds of ermines living in the lath.

The Gambler

Yasha's coat hangs on the broken pedestal.
It is unobtrusive, like Yasha, homeless
and deeply suggestive of ploys, but resigned
as an octopus to waiting.
It is the second day of spring.
Yesterday a young woman brought a paper of daffodils.
They cup out in the dark room.
New York hums through the brick walls.
Down in the brick well interior court of garbage,
below the window, screams of a child.
Intermittent, continuous as Morse code,
the calling of cars and sirens in the deep flow,
like the music of whales.
Yasha sits in his borrowed room
and fiddles with a magnetic chessboard.
He has come from Moscow via Tel Aviv
to play the game. He speaks Russian
and Hebrew; mispronouncing a little English.
In his pocket, photographs of men bent
over chessboards. A harsh light
casts their faces in severe abstract designs.

Incarnation

Every day a woman stands in her kitchen
and listens to a bird.
It is the voice of her dead husband,
only now he has wings and sings
to another female sitting on a nest.

Inaccurate. Incarnation is only
a twin maze on empty glass.
Meat is the measure.
But every day Belshazzar
leaves strange writings on the windows.
Every night passes grief-stricken, weeping.

Incarnation is an empty glass.
Meat is the measure.
But every day Belshazzar
makes strange markings in the dust.
Every night her bed sinks into the earth.
Every day she cooks and eats
and then, washes the dirty dishes.

The woman wishes it could be otherwise.
She would like to be a bird;
for her kingdom to perish;
for the house to fall down.

This Strangeness in My Life

It is so hard to see where it is,
but it is there even in the morning
when the miracle of shapes
assemble and become familiar,
but not quite; and the echo
of a voice, now changed,
utterly dissociated, as though
all warmth and shared sweetness
had never been. It is this alien
space, not stark as the moon,
but lush and almost identical
to the space that was. But it is not.
It is another place and you are not
what you were but as though emerging
from the air, you slowly show yourself
as someone else, not ever remembered.

Genesis

Cylinder sacks of water filling the oceans,
endless bullets of water,
skins full of water rolling and tumbling
as we came together.
As though light broke us apart.
As though light came with the rubble of words,
though we die among the husks of remembering.
It is as we knew it would be
in the echoes of endless terminals,
in the slow scaled guises of ourselves
when we came together in the envelopes of ourselves,
the bare shadow, the breath of words invisible;
as slight errors repeating themselves;
as degradation passes like madness through a crowd.
It was not ordained.
It was one drop of salt water against another.

White on White

A white cobra lily,
oyster-white plaster walls,
a glass of Chablis.

Parchment-white old woman's piss,
light on the grains of moisture,
the grains of wax.

The stoma, trembling in its enclosure,
white cells, white continents.

Heavy white pear bottoms,
the bellies of Lytton
Strachey and Queen Victoria.

White mucus from healthy vaginas,
white straps, white girdles,
white satin trims of the bride's
lingerie made in Hong Kong.

White parasites, white peacocks, white amanitas.

Shapes

In the longer view it doesn't matter.
However, it's that having lived, it matters.
So that every death breaks you apart.
You find yourself weeping at the door
of your own kitchen, overwhelmed
by loss. And you find yourself weeping
as you pass the homeless person
head in hands resigned on a cement
step, the wire basket on wheels right there.
Like stopped film, or a line of Vallejo,
or a sketch of the mechanics of a wing
by Leonardo. All pauses in space,
a violent compression of meaning
in an instant within the meaningless.
Even staring into the dim shapes
at the farthest edge; accepting that blur.

Entering the Student's Poem

The most beautiful videos
come from reading poetry.
And they're in your head.
How many times you speak
to the woman wrapped in a black shawl;
how many times you go up to her
where she sits on the bench
near the railroad, alone, waiting.
But she speaks no English
and the tall girl you have become;
your straight blond hair in a Grecian bun,
your voice melodious, shaking,
because the language is so difficult,
because you are traveling alone;
all this comes to you
from three or four lines
written by a student
who always sits midway in the class;
smiling if you call on her,
the blood rushing to her forehead.

Changes

Say, 7-Eleven where some guy
uses a newspaper to cover it.
(Holds it in his left hand.)
Just an ordinary stickup.
Did 7-Eleven close down?
Don't think so; dunno.
Money won't change
the way that word guy changed.
On stereoscopic cards
you view this regular
good time guy. He wears
a linen suit and a Panama hat.
There he is waving it
from a trolley attached to a guy wire.
There the trolley goes, stuffed
with the Baptist church on a picnic.
Those summer trollies, open sides,
woven bamboo seats;
driver clanging the bell,
single set of tracks, inter-urban,
swooshing the chicory.
And someone along the way
is sure to say, "Whoa there,
you guys."
At which they all lift their Panamas
and the ladies laugh.
Well, here it is past eleven,
my feet hanging over the side

of a single bed. Out there
this deep lake, a mere memory;
the open mouth of a glacier
one mile thick, a big stickup
that melted during the interim
warm spell, after it gouged
the bedrock down to a whisper
and filled it with recycled water;
rimmed with the teeth of conifers
whose seeds are ancient, cunning
and guileful; successful guys so far…

March 15, 1998

Let me forget
when the hanged man
looks in the window.
Outside, the desperate
speak in a lost language.
Let us in, they sigh,
with the tongues of waterfalls.
But you, out of breath,
category of the misplaced;
serial-killer of my days;
while my left ventricle
pumps the exact pressure
of the universe…
in spite of your default,
with no substantial reason,
I speak for you
as though you are still here.
We are arranged like that.
A sad mistake, a Mandelbrot,
a fractal glitch, a gift from zero.

Visions from My Office Window

Among the students between the buildings,
the colors of their clothes is a mirage of tulips.
The lash of hot and cold upstate
New York mountain weather;
April splinters like an ice palace.
And among them, one who looks
like a Sicilian widow; is this a new beginning
or is she bringing food for the daughter?
If so, the daughter will likely spurn it.
"Mama," she'll say, "go back to the kitchen.
Leave me alone." The widow shrugs and passes
with the stream of students. She is
very likely a student herself just trying on
one of her multiple guises, the black cape,
the wrapped shawl; hurrying by herself,
prematurely old, carrying a basket of produce,
her eyes deep-set and dark as olives.

The Illusion

I am not the genes and the genes are not me.
We are identical twins, separated at birth.
This is my sinew. This is my fertile ovary.
What is worth the universe is also worth me.

I am not me. I am the genes. The double helix.
My future is spelled out. Tool of the universe:
pricks, cunts, genuflections; the orgasm's curse,
brief span, holy thou: I am the neutron fix.

I am the hole, the dark other, the negative between
I was and I am. Wherefore yes, dense and disperse,
blinded visionary that locks the moon in place;
I am the simple sieve that drinks the universe.

Again—Now

This vague surreal cityscape,
not get-at-able; neither clear
nor cloudy; still bare, although
the tips are splitting, and origami
wrinkled packages of birthing,
verdigris squeezing out, and drips
of sugar water; the thin milk
of each bud-ovary, waxy,
with the tensile strength of steel.
These extruding lungs,
the summer's vast breathing;
the blood of cambium mixing its gases
with the blood of meat bodies;
the resuscitation promised
season after season, more and more
like the paramedic breathing into
the heart-stopped victim; the victim
stretched unconscious on the sidewalk,
the savior with the fix leaning into
and sucking the dead back
to the difficult, even impossible,
even dreaded and unwanted quick.

The Electric Fan and The Dead Man
(or the widow as a useful object toward the end
of the century)

She remembers his covert sleeves,
the sadness of his quiet.

Still, there is the unplugged fan
staring at the floor
with the nonexpression of the working class
temporarily laid off;
ignorant of where its wild pulsating energy comes from,
like the former ideal woman,
ready to serve you right up,
and then, the flipping eyebrows,
the gesture of wringing hands.

He lies folding into himself.
Was it the velvet vest that gave him such gravity?
She thinks, looking back,
that he was the product of his time,
the first half of that section up through the fifties.
While she is more like the fan, sighing her way into the last half;
more useful now than then… to stir the air, i.e.,
the projected rise in temperatures
and boiling in your own sweat… etc.
(A slight up, Fahrenheit-wise,
of the blood, and its zap.)

The fan, ready for service, bent neck, sans bathrobe,
or, for all that, sans torso; really just a head;
but still, something oiled about the skin,

although stiff enough,
ready to smile
without implying anything original
or shocked – more than one would be by
sticking a pinky into a wall socket.

What is imperative is the Off switch;
which he, at one point some time ago,
opted for himself.
Tied a silk cord around his meat neck
and hung his meat body, loved though it was,
in order to insure absolute quiet,
on the back of a rented door in Soho.
And on a certain level that did it.
But as for her, to mix the metaphor,
she continues, having once read Huysmans in the original,
ready for, at least mechanically, *fin de siècle, à rebours.*

As It Is

In this squat body,
the most delicate things;
host of ravishing flagella.
Out of the Far East,
dormant diseases
waiting their turn.
The cavity under the skull
not proliferating
but shoring up, shrinking.
Outside, the air, lightly
polluted as everywhere;
the crime rate steady
and rising. Oh, world,
I said, feeling with my feet
her soft pubic hair,
the uncut grass outside
my kitchen door,
her benign pulse hot
on my skin, the apple trees'
spent petals letting go
in the slight wind, gyrating
down like snow. Oh world, I said.

Useless Words

Taste and smell of rain
and beyond the veil,
your voice,
its trembling undertones
without body or remorse;
these hours
that keep me as an ornament.

Even the ocean's largess
lies flat without resonance.
Your voice still
beating inside my skull,
as if I could put my fingers
through my eyes and pull you out.
This dumb external universe.

Those commonplace things,
coffee and toast;
then we had nothing but streets,
the city trees; lived in rented rooms.
Why does your body odor
retain such violence;
your ordinary shirts
become cloth of lamé, bitter flowers?

The Eye within the Eye

I am intimate with the black square
eye sockets of two computers.
I know, but they do not, that
I am not the Abyssinian crouched
on the windowsill.
But time by battery rules here.
It flashes in the history of violence,
this wiring of the world.
As yet, it does not compute the fabulous gnat,
or squid, all brain, brilliant and tactile.
And out there under the cement,
the nematodes are rising from the dead.

Always on the Train

Writing poems about writing poems
is like rolling bales of hay in Texas.
Nothing but the horizon to stop you.

But consider the railroad's edge of metal trash;
bird perches, miles of telephone wires.
What is so innocent as grazing cattle?
If you think about it, it turns into words.

Trash is so cheerful, flying up
like grasshoppers in front of the reaper.
The dust devil whirls it aloft: bronze candy wrappers,
squares of clear plastic — windows on a house of air.

Below the weedy edge in last year's mat,
red and silver beer cans.
In bits blown equally everywhere,
the gaiety of flying paper
and the black high flung patterns of flocking birds.

Bits of Information

While her minuscule fledglings, each slightly
larger and heavier than a bumblebee,
are rising out of the woven handbag of their nest,
this hummingbird is sipping jewelweed.
It's all that's left. She should be at magenta
and scarlet, not this small orange and yellow
flowering lip. The jewelweed shoots its seeds
with buckshot energy. Its chemistry once used
to soothe the blisters etched by poison ivy.
The female hummingbird is heavier than he
and darker without the ruby at the throat.
Still hovering in air, her wing beats blur invisible.
While he, a smaller body, father of the fledglings,
has gone free; an irresponsible bachelor
since that quick act of sex; her single parenting
is adequate. The fledglings emulate and follow her.
This winged woman Icarus never dreamed of,
will cross the Gulf of Mexico, living on stored up fat.

A Woodchuck Lesson

To reach the University,
you park your car on Rapist Hill
and walk slipping over fallen sweet-gum leaves
to a shared cubicle.
You're hired for the year.
In the evening, ten miles back to Earlysville.
Since renting this tin-roofed farmhouse
from a cattle broker who lives in town,
these long weekends on the dry acreage
you study the worn-out fields,
chicory-starred stubble.
The buzzards in their ecological niche
always there, circling.
The house, two hundred years old,
has no veranda.
A small graveyard from that early time,
boundaries marked with rough quartz,
fallen headstones, faded names and dates.
What lies here were young women and infants:
a year by year ledger of replacements.
In contrast, the new back steps,
almost flush to the door;
like the ready-made entrance to a trailer.
You sit here. Doves throttle;
dragonflies, blue against blue.
A bird, in quick parabolas,
swoops in and out of the walnut tree.
The great drouth-struck walnut, its maternal shade,

green compound tiny heart-shaped leaves,
the leaves cutting their losses,
fluttering loose,
stripping the branches naked.
While the cattle
gather at the gate;
strings of glistening spittle,
ruminating empty cuds, uneasy shuffling.
A woodchuck lives under the shed.
On the dirt road, only rednecks;
guns across the back windows of their pickup trucks.
Still, things being as they are,
the woodchuck has a back door
and sometimes you see her sitting on her stoop,
warming herself in the sun;
her fat belly, her paws resting on her front
like a grandmother.
Then her quick over and under
when nearby penned-up hounds
yammer and bay.
She seems old and devious.
Not like these ear-clipped, blue-stamped,
condemned cattle who are starving on thin grass,
who huddle near the fence, near the loading ramp.

Marbles

Or again, agates,
milk blue and glass filled,
a cloudy universe.
Not so much a game
as a sphere,
a mystery.
Held up to light,
a small hole
into another dimension.

Or again,
living in the center
of a worn-out Southern farm,
renting the old house,
surrounded by uncultivated fields
now owned by a cattle broker
who buys up the substandard
cattle at auctions
and pastures them on quack grass,
a temporary holding place,
a pause to browse on chicory.
In this place you learn
about freezers by osmosis.
How beef halves are hung,
how nothing is overlooked,
not even the great globes
of fly stung eyes, gouged out
and washed of blood;
round and milky blue as marbles.

Eyes, most desperately your own,
fading from over-use,
and in the wear of night long
burning bulbs, the constant light;
reading and falling asleep
and waking to read.

Strange imagined shapes of things,
wild distortions of the familiar,
like the galaxies, pinpoints
of the imagined; until
the polished multiple eyes
of lofted telescopes –
while buffeted by cosmic dust
and plasma –
passed down bit by bit
the great glass marble of the universe.

Parts of Speech

Flight of verbs outstretched,
muscular extrusion.
Yet, no more than Betelgeuse
or geese, up from an oil spill,
wedge askew.
Probability against stasis.
It's a dirty self-cleaning universe.
Our problem is:
are we scum or sediment?
Every action has a reaction.
It's a Mandelbrot.
It's a trap.
It's our excuse.

Before the Blight

The elms stretched themselves in indolent joy,
arching over the street that lay in green shadow
under their loose tent.
And the roses in Mrs. Mix's yard pretzeled up her trellis
with pink Limoges cabbage blooms like Rubens' nudes.
My lips whispered over the names of things
in the meadows, in the orchard, in the woods,
where I sometimes stood for long moments
listening to some bird telling me of the strangeness of myself;
rocked in the sinewy arms of summer.

Poems

When you come back to me
it will be crow time
and flycatcher time,
with rising spirals of gnats
between the apple trees.
Every weed will be quadrupled,
coarse, welcoming
and spine-tipped.
The crows, their black flapping
bodies, their long calling
toward the mountain;
relatives, like mine,
ambivalent, eye-hooded;
hooting and tearing.
And you will take me in
to your fractal meaningless
babble; the quick of my mouth,
the madness of my tongue.

What Meets the Eye

Trash in the yards
white as early flowers,
the flash of aluminum cans
in broad sweeps
spilling down the embankments
to the shelter of rusty bedsprings
and the creosote fat of old tires,
the brawl of oil drums.
Now and again, the bold spread
of a car dump fans out,
then closes with the single shell
of an orange Vega, fastened
like a mutant insect to the slope.

Something almost yields.
It's that week before the flush of shoots
and the blue rush of Texas wild flowers.
Hawks on the updraft;
pockets of sky reflecting water.
It's that season of unreasoning hope,
when flocks of starlings
pulse up in a single motion,
then scatter like a handful of grain
flung out over the fields.

Junction in the Midwest

If we look back
it grabs our attention;
that woman on the platform
in a nice white dress
and wide-brimmed hat
with her hand up, holding
the sun away from her eyes.
As the train pulls out
she is dramatically alone,
looking up and down the track.
Miles further on a voice
over the intercom repeats
a name, saying, "If you are
on the train, please see
the conductor." We sway on
with no pause at small stations.
By now the expectant woman
has probably gone home
to check her messages.
Perhaps the expected one,
snoring with mouth open,
is still slumped in a rear seat
traveling relentlessly toward
Chicago. The flat fields
stretch to the rim. One child
sees a pig and is so pleased
her mother tells us about it.
Low rectangular warehouses

along the track, small dusty towns,
farm machines, and parking lots
with bright colored cars exactly
spaced. Then nothing but gray
pollution-blue sky, fractured clouds
like cotton wipes, and the upright
tassels of field corn, mile after mile.

Breathing

By day the brook is subsumed
under a rush of summer;
voices of motors and warblers,
rubbing steel of the swings;
the shouting across the road
for dogs, for children.
Even when you go down to its bed,
it gives way to this busy noise.

A gang of crows and everything's
overhead; chipping sparrows,
spin of their stubborn trills;
slip of the maples tangled
together; great mops scrubbing
the air; the slosh of wind.

But at night, the water lipping
below the voice of your breathing,
or the catch of your breath,
its stopped stillness; when
you wake with a start and listen
for the sound of the spill
beginning again, braiding itself,
and the fall of rock on rock
sucked down in its liquid mouth.

On the Slow Train Passing Through

Here's Moody Furniture and the town of Moody. Also the display
for Temple Chemicals, a wire fence, some rubble and bare ground.
Privy to this endless street along the tracks, I watch
ongoing traffic move around something in the road.
It's a man on the center line lying on his back;
a woman bending down to touch him.
The cars move on. The train slides past.
And yet, in Roanoke, Virginia, in 1907, when grandma's
house was on fire, the passing trolley stopped and everyone
got off and ran up the hill to help, even though there was no easy water.
Three members of a Baptist choir endangered their whiskers,
their business attires, their waistcoats and themselves, to carry
out grandma's organ and her cherry sitting room furniture.
Although the upstairs burned through the roof and my mother's
new treadle sewing machine and her new tailored suit were
among the traumatic losses; they all did what they could.
It was the dignity of a communal disaster. No one was going
anywhere more important than that. The trolley horse had been
unhitched and loosely tethered to graze and eventually they heard
the far off sound of the approaching fire brigade. Meanwhile,
grandpa had been fetched from the foundry. Afterward, those women
who had done all they could to save my grandma's belongings,
total strangers, each in her own way commiserated with grandma.
The men washed at the pump and they all walked down the hill.
The conductor hitched up the trolley and they went on with their
     regular day.

Eden, Then and Now

In '29 before the dust storms
sandblasted Indianapolis,
we believed in the milk company.
Milk came in glass bottles.
We spread dye-colored butter,
now connected to cancer.
We worked seven to seven
with no overtime pay;
pledged allegiance every day,
pitied the starving Armenians.
One morning in the midst of plenty,
there were folks out of context,
who were living on nothing.
Some slept in shacks
on the banks of the river.
This phenomenon investors said
would pass away.
My father worked for the daily paper.
He was a union printer;
lead slugs and blue smoke.
He worked with hot lead
at a two-ton machine,
in a low-slung seat;
a green-billed cap
pulled low on his forehead.
He gave my mother a dollar a day.
You could say we were rich.
This was the Jazz Age.

All over the country
the dispossessed wandered
with their hungry children,
harassed by the law.
When the market broke, bad losers
jumped out of windows.
It was time to lay an elegant table,
as it is now; corporate paradise;
the apple before the rot caved in.
It was the same worm
eating the same fruit.
In fact, the same Eden.

Wanting

Wanting and dissatisfaction
are the main ingredients
of happiness.
To want is to believe
there is something worth getting.
Whereas getting only shows
how worthless the thing is.
And this is why destruction
is so useful.
It gets rid of what was wanted
and so makes room
for more to be wanted.
How valueless is the orderly.
It cries out for disorder.
And life that thinks it fears death,
spends all of its time
courting death.
To violate beauty
is the essence of sexual desire.
To procreate is the essence of decay.

Don't Miss It

If you're looking for a heron on one leg,
or a white egret in this water-logged parcel;
you may be blind to boarded-up gas pumps,
flashes of sleazy mock-up towns;
though finally, a rusted roof,
gaping shed or wizened trailer,
may appear like strange fowl;
as you snake on past dry bayous
where the old jalopies flake to crust,
splintering their jumping joy-juice;
battered bodies, the good old boys left behind.

At the Ready

Under the aerial squadron,
wheat fields are ready
for McCormick reapers.
The planes pass over
copulating mice;
grasshoppers, programmed like
investors on the margin;
ants, relocating tons of soil;
and snakes with useful toads
still kicking in their guts.
These items are not among
the criteria for observation.

From overhead, the planes,
geometrically spaced,
cast long stippled shadows
on the rippling fields;
dark flashes like a military code,
like an urgent monotonous message
beamed to the combat zone,
repeating instructions to the already dead.

That Other War

A bird sings in the tree you planted
beside your stamped-out storage barn,
plastic barn that fits all over
America in three sizes; the bird does not know
that you have gone away, worker of puzzles,
hero of the Philippines. You who wanted
no more than flower beds, zoysia grass,
a round of golf. Years passed
before you told us that after laying down
the communication lines, you returned
to find them all ambushed; torsos
severed. Some had no faces.
After the war it seemed the war
in the head didn't end so easily.
In the night you would try to choke
your wife and she would wake you up.
But even that passes.

This bird sings for itself
a soft unconscious mourning.
Your wife hears it but does not
know that she is listening.
Her collection of figurines
still on the shelves you built
for them and she is still
working in this grocery and that,
handing out coupons and samples.

Tip of the Iceberg

The forests of the world are disappearing.
Recent photographs show
vast bald areas in Vermont,
the Amazon, Brazil, and so forth.
There is a growing suspicion among some of us
that the lumbermen and the lumber industries
are in reality outsized carpenter ants.
The genuine original ants having tunneled
into these once human but now ants' brains,
are operating there
as from the cab of a multipositional
all functions destructo-bulldozer.
These large live robots
are ant machines.
They are breaking ground for an ant
takeover.
This far-seeing project
has been vaguely apprehended
by satellite.

Napping on the Greyhound

It's Christmas Eve in Texas.
Your bored self is outside the bus
running barefoot on the red shale.
The bus wheezes with the slushy road.
Sage and collapsed yucca, snow snagged
on the barbed-wire fences;
you close one eye.
Outside leaping over boulders,
your bored self stares in at itself sleeping.
The big-headed yucca, helpless as fresh born,
are uncovered in the blizzard.
They are quiet as baby birds.
"Inscrutable inhabitants," say shy visitors
from Planet Zizz. "Very tasteful antennae."

Reading the Russians

Of course they are gloomy;
they drink a lot of vodka.
It's a frost bitten country.
The women are trivialized,
used, thrown aside. It's a gambler's code.
This is not even subliminal.
All those Victorian translations
where I was transfixed:
lying stomach down on my bed
that summer of my fourteenth year,
a library book flat under my right thumb,
slant of sun moment by moment
across the window, my heart rushing
with the wolves, the exhausted horses,
the over-turned sleighs,
the cold veil of the Steppes.
And then reaching deep
into their Mongolian survival,
the harsh Cossack law, the saber;
the mud and stick quadrangles.
And the Ukraine, where the mammoths grazed,
the length of which the Arctic birds
crossed in early summer,
their undulating shadows blotting out the light;
or grasshoppers in clouds arose
as if from the shattering of meteors
rebounding in phosphorescent flashes;
where the sinews of the saber-toothed

and the white leopard were buried beneath
the slow accruing rubble and on top of that,
Chernobyl, and Gogol's nose.

What We Have

On the mountain
the neighbor's dog, put out in the cold,
comes to my house for the night.
He quivers with gratitude.
His short-haired small stout body
settles near the stove.
He snores.
Out there in the dark, snow falls.
The birch trees are wrapped in their white bandages.
Recently in the surgical theater,
I looked in the mirror at the doctor's hands
as he repaired my ancient frescos.
When I was ten
we lived in a bungalow in Indianapolis.
My sister and brother, my mother and father,
all living then.
We were like rabbits
in the breast fur of a soft lined nest.
I know now we were desperately poor.
But it was spring:
the field, a botanist's mirage of wild flowers.
The house centered between two railroad tracks.
The tracks split at the orchard end of the street
and spread in a dangerous angle down either side.
Long lines of freight for half an hour clicking by;
or a passenger train,
with a small balcony at the end of the last car
where someone always stood and waved to us.

At night the wrenching scream and Doppler whistle
of the two AM express.
From my window I could see a fireman stoking
the open fire, the red glow reflected in the black smoke
belching from the boiler.
Once I got up and went outside.
The trees-of-heaven along the track swam in white mist.
The sky arched with sickle pears.
Lilacs had just opened.
I pulled the heavy clusters to my face
and breathed them in,
suffused with a strange excitement
that I think, when looking back, was happiness.

A Pair

The black and white cat
means to get off
the screened-in porch.
Castrated but suave,
he lives with this older woman
whose husband, dead thirty years,
secretly puts his cheek to hers
in a dime store photograph.
The children no longer visit.
The cat holds all the threads
of her detonated psyche.
He is the master key without
a lock. She picks him up.
The porch screen has been mended.
He thinks there are the old openings.
Birds, insects leap
out of the flecked light.
Inside the screen, her hands
stroke his electric body.

Spring Snow

Rain of remembering;
late snow turning to rain.
Then in the cold house,
alone in bed,
the soft stutter on the roof,
random phrases; your voice,
only your voice. How can
it be that voice that touched
me everywhere?
And what you said,
if only I could hear it again
in its intensity.
Essence distilled
in the moment of waking,
the delicate mold and odors
of the breaking apart of winter,
in the soft snow that comes
between the past and the chill
distillation, the whisper of air
split between the perfume
of melting crystals; the clasp
and letting go.

What We Don't Know

It is Wednesday. My day off.
The neighborhood quiet.
My cats pulse, tails up,
like submarines scanning the surface.
Last night through the lifted window,
melting snow released an ozone sting.
Last night I twisted in the arms
of a heavy book on radioactive pollution.
I have gone through its troubled corridors.
In its inner labyrinths, I have eaten
the survivors, the mutilated bodies,
the cancers of children; like fruitcake
sliced in the kitchen at 3 AM;
all this only whets the appetite;
the insomniac leaning
against the doorjamb.
Now it's 11 AM on Wednesday;
the area, ordinary, as usual.
Fog beads along the wires.
Last night's implant in the brain,
useless information after the facts,
like the gradual glitch of shifting faults,
almost unnoticed; in the way
two birds streak through the air,
in the wing language of April,
above them the dark metaphor
of two soundless fighter jets.

Linear Illusions

Some days seem significant.
Premature lacewings hatch in the house.
Crawling over vast wastes of plastic
they fly toward light.
Outside, snow is crusted. Inside,
insects programmed in perfection –
on the wrong side of the window.

This evening Cabernet Sauvignon,
mushroom omelette.
Outside, rain has brought up worms.
They lie exhausted in straight lines.
Some are drowned.
Narrow and pink at either end,
they cannot decide which direction.

I have decided on blank pages.
In them you can travel forever;
white flying toward your eyes;
as when driving through falling snow
you see only those snowflakes
you are cutting across;
relentlessly horizontal.

When I Was Thirty-five You Took My Photograph

I am lying full length on the grass,
turned toward you,
resting on hip and elbow,
my cheek
against the spread fingers
of my left hand.
It is midsummer.
My breasts are pendulous,
my eyes half open;
a damp sheen of sweat
highlights my face
that is more naked
than my naked body.
My stomach is flat.
There is a fine torque
between my waist
and my hip bone.
In your darkroom
where you often disappeared,
a blank in the calendar,
the film would lie in an acid bath,
the negative then scrutinized,
washed and hung, like our sheets,
with ordinary clothespins.
Evenings, you bent over the enlarger.
Dispassionate, I consider
this photograph.
You were influenced
by Modigliani's nudes.

Love

This part of myself devoted to you
admits of nothing that falls away.
Although I melt moment by moment
into something else, I carry you
with me, a doll of circumstance,
that dances as I do when I
present myself, the stranger,
to you, the stranger. We speak
of them hurriedly. We
take them out of our breasts
and hold them out to each other,
the glass hearts, the transparent bodies.

To Give This a Name, Astonishing

Since the weather is mine, or the window,
even the separation from the weather,
it is my body, only my body, that knows
this weather. Whatever shapes those crystals
fit, edges connect, they coalesce, fall,
agglomerate, and change in fragile patterns,
original, infinite as this continuum, whatever.
I see the veil of illusions, the momentum
into which I may thrust my arm, hand, fingers,
to feel from the couplers and nerve endings
my heat glowing out from me, crushing their
geometric inventions, the silent click of crystals
fracturing. At this moment thinking that the shapes
of starfish, along a similar lattice, reflect another
pattern of angles crossing and recrossing within
the magnet of an invisible circle. The weather
fills my lungs, is allowed by the multiple corporation
of my interlocking cells to conjoin within the oceans
and abysses of this fabulous puzzle and I become
the weather as it becomes me, as water, the enabler,
mirage of pattern, illusion of vapor, snowfall,
even the window, all fractals become conjured out of chaos.

Reality

As a fish, gutted for trade,
so my darling as a cadaver
was slit, his viscera removed;
pulled out by a gloved hand
as waste; the still pulsing
microscopic flagella,
only recently going about its business
in the small scape of the veins,
the glut of the great esophagus
and the first bend of the squirming bowel.
He who was so lovely
with his dark brows and hawk-like nose,
his teeth, irregular from childhood poverty,
or those mobile and compassionate lips
through which he breathed
sweet deadly smoke and words.
The absurd corpse, its now useless testicles
hung below that flaccid thing,
that limp thumb of shriveled skin.
All that sprang up in him so mortal,
so beautiful; come to this.

At Eighty-three She Lives Alone

Enclosure, steam-heated; a trial casket.
You are here; your name on a postal box;
entrance into another place like vapor.
No one knows you. No one speaks to you.
All of their cocks stare down their pant legs
at the ground. Their cunts are blind. They
barely let you through the check-out line.
Have a nice day. Plastic or paper?

Are you origami? A paper folded swan,
like the ones you made when you were ten?
When you saw the constellations, lying
on your back in the wet grass,
the soapy pear blossoms drifting
and wasting, and those stars, the burned out ones
whose light was still coming in waves;
your body was too slight.
How could it hold such mass?
Still on your lips the taste of something.

All night you waited for morning, all morning
for afternoon, all afternoon for night;
and still the longing sings.
Oh, paper bird with folded wings.

A Good Question

Look at these disparate shapes.
The air is displaced
by the bulk of the table.
The table is borrowed.
For that matter, the chair is plastic.
Altogether, the square room
is concealed from the snow.
The snow falls for nine hours.
Occasionally on the sly
I raise up the window.
An implosion of temperatures
condenses steam to water.
How can I live like this?

Getting to Know You

We slept into one another.
The mattress sloped us to your side.
We shared three daughters.
Miraculous dull day to day
breakfast and dinner.

But compared to all the optic scanning,
the nerve ends of retrospection
in my thirty years of knowing you
cell by cell in my widow's shawl,
we have lived together longer
in the discontinuous films of my sleep
than we did in our warm parasitical bodies.

Thus, by comparison, when the palms
of our hands lay together exchanging oils
and minuscule animals of the skin;
we were relative strangers.

From Boston to Binghamton

It's not that looking at the ceiling
of a bus depot delivers wisdom,
but aside from the emergency
exit and the sober down-to-earth
driver, we seem to have lifts
on our wheels. It's the purple
clusters of insect landing fields,
the spread out lips of roseate
horticultural specimens,
those shameless lures
the father of genetics
never dreamed of.
But, oh, in this work-a-day world
where factual is fractal and
everything leads to something
else and division is beyond
control, the great moving mass
of us is on the road, unblinking
mirage; getting from here to
there in the intense purpose that
we must fulfill. Strange
superficial gauze; slipping stroke
and burning center of the veil.

Air

Through the open window, a confusion
of gasoline fumes, lilacs, the green esters of grass.
Edward Waite rides the lawn mower.
Each summer his voice is more stifled. His emphysema is worse.
"Three packs a day," he says, still proud of the fact.
Before he got sick, he drove semis across the country.
Every two weeks he drives his small truck up the mountain.
He mows in long rows fitting swath to cut swath, overlapping the width.
To please me he saves the wild paintbrush along the edge.
Stripped to the waist, I see he has hung his blue shirt
on my clothesline to dry out the sweat.
The shirt, with its arms upraised, filled with the body of air,
is deeply inhaling, exhaling its doppelgänger breath.

Sorrow and No Sorrow

We eat through tubes of time
as the cockroach,
as the apple and the codling moth,
as worms of neutrinos;
and what is not there
is always more than there.
As the dropped fawn,
dappled and cinnamon;
as the wind lays the fern aside
and carries the fawn's milk breath
over the ravenous field
on its indifferent tongue.

Points of Vision

In February the hills of Niguel flush green,
a rush of new grass fine as baby hair.
Shizu drives out with her easel.
The red-tailed hawks are working
the folds and wrinkles where
the ground squirrels hide.
Tormented by crows, three hawks
spiral up and drift under and over,
becoming small as sparrows.
Above them a jet streaks in the cumulus.
Frenetic ground squirrels
pop in and out of their burrows.
Now they're motionless.
Now the enlarged shadow
of a descending hawk
sweeps over the hummocks,
like a blind hand feeling its way.
Shizu prepares her watercolors.

Train Ride

All things come to an end;
small calves in Arkansas,
the bend of the muddy river.
Do all things come to an end?
No, they go on forever.
They go on forever, the swamp,
the vine-choked cypress, the oaks
rattling last year's leaves,
the thump of the rails, the kite,
the still white stilted heron.
All things come to an end.
The red clay bank, the spread hawk,
the bodies riding this train,
the stalled truck, pale sunlight, the talk;
the talk goes on forever,
the wide dry field of geese,
a man stopped near his porch
to watch. Release, release;
between cold death and a fever,
send what you will, I will listen.
All things come to an end.
No, they go on forever.

Assumptions

That you seem to be this voice,
these eyes,
this poundage of upright snail
is always, when examined,
somewhat suspicious.
The inner is really the outer.
And again, you are reminded
of the Klein bottle.

The Poem

Exactly at three PM
it came walking in
with blocks of wood in its arms.
I was building a table on the patio.
Could I refuse?
The wood smelled of mold,
old saw cuts, sawdust.
It began in the arteries, rushing.
Words without words.
Looking down I saw last year's leaves
in pockets and nests of humus
between the flagstones.
The warblers and thrushes sang
clear of the maggots.
Everything knew
it was too soon to die.
Even the old maple
that had been struck by lightning.
Then it passed by
like a cold breath.

The Interesting Way of Life

Hard of hearing, I kept the National Public
Radio station on "Too loud," she said.
She watched TV in the room above my bed.
I read all night.

My dog dirtied the backyard. Because of this,
she hung her laundry up there on her balcony.
Her Olds was pristine white, second-hand, in good condition.
She was neat, fat, religious.

I worried about her opinion.
I thought, "Here we are."
One day I saw her on crutches. One day she cried.
Her job was at risk. She thought she might lose her car.

Her mother came.
They were two hot-air balloons.
They were a pair of enormous Kewpie dolls.
It was all the same.

Although I tried;
she went back to upstaging me.
She belonged to the Neighborhood Watch. She went to church.
Her cats were immortal. My dog died.

The Provider

Several crows were lined up along the ridge of a quite ordinary house. "These ridge poles are a good idea," said a young one. "Who dreamed it up?" "This place of rest is a fortuitous gift from the moon," said a raven who was mixing with the hoi polloi today. "The moon is a relative of the roc, a distant cousin of mine. Believe me," he said, stretching his wings out to their full advantage and pushing the crows at the end off balance, so several leaped into the wind and cried "caw"... "it depends on your original stock. I've got a piece of the roc." The moon rose spectral and drained, a gossamer imprint of her nighttime self, a reminder of crystal fracture, the load of swinging primitive stones, the ancient hairy arms with slingshots. A sudden explosion and the sky was defined with flapping and cawing. "What was that?" cried the young one who was addicted to awe. "Who knows?" replied the raven. "Often the moon demands a sacrifice. As a close relative, it is now my duty to go and eat the meat. For it is said, nothing is wasted; nothing is without purpose." And the raven rose and flew toward the hunters.

Surviving

I speak to you who are still loath to answer,
out of the flagella of my cells. I hear distant flutterings,
bird whistles and the sky's wet slough
dissolving into fragments, shadows that were.

You who are always sinking into must,
stripping back, the gaud of skeletons,
cum of molecules, kiss of gas;
the exact never to be repeated form gone slack.

Now it is spring. Again it is that time you hung yourself.
Which self among you silenced all the rest?
Your psyche splintered selves, one for each year;
myself, who was, went with you into dust.

Now I am the simple who rose up and lived;
each day a blank, each night a catacomb.

Light

The house across the way
facing east, light clips it,
girdles it.
Parting the veil,
morning is the husband.
The rose nipple of the chimney;
leaded windows like painted lashes;
a subtle odor of lip wax.
Without a key, light enters
with its hot blond muzzle
and lies upon the body;
and the body stirs and remembers.

Drought

For weeks, no rain.
If the sun does not leap
in a dance of veils
to make the wired veins of the sky
chortle and rasp like an old man
in his bed crying for women,
then the brook will run dry.
This matter of pebbles and boulders
will mark the place;
this moraine of old sockets,
skulls of deer mice,
wing joints of wood thrushes,
claws of the veery unclasped
from the branch where the notes decayed.
It will go on like this: no trace of black flies,
no nymphs walking on water.

Sorrow

Living alone the feet turn voluptuous,
cold as sea water, the thin brine
of the blood reaches them slowly;
their nubby heads rub one another.
How can you love them and yet
how live without them?
Their shoes lined up like caskets
in which they lie all day
dead from one another.
In the night
each foot has nothing to love
but the other foot.

Albany Bus Station

The same fat man with the fluorescent vest
is playing cards for cash
at the same table by the window;
the same easy jean-jacketed girl
slaps the back of the same red-faced man
whose shirt hangs out below his sweater.
And the same dusky man joins the game,
angry as before — ready to shout and throw
his deal down. It's the everyday crowd
that comes in when the mesh gates
are pulled back and the lunch line
offers chicken wings and gravy.
I'm here, too, in my moon boots from Ames,
my pink quilted coat, holding this brocaded
handbag lumpy with face cream, toothpaste,
bottles of vitamins, carbon receipts,
a plastic bag of quarters, and my dime-store
glasses. My poems and books
are in the borrowed suitcase under the table.
I'm sitting here with the small
cup of decaf, watching them play cards.
I am homeless. I forget who I am
or where I was before I got here.
For two hours I am in their avant-garde
drama by Beckett. I am nowhere.
Until outside the window, the big ultra-real
green and white Vermont Transit Bus
pulls in to take me home to Brandon.

Cousin Francis Speaks Out

Buddy's uncle Hiram felt bad about his sister, Mable.
Hiram always had a good job with the railroad.
He'd come out and give Buddy a few dollars once a month.
Mable was Buddy's ma. She had seven living
and they were all boys.
Buddy took care of his ma
when she come home from the insane asylum.
He drove a Holsum Bread truck.
He had a place of his own,
three rooms and toilet with cement floor.
Mable was in the asylum twenty-five years
on account of chopping up the furniture
when Shafe, her shiftless run-around old man,
tossed the baby up against the ceiling
and then it died of brain fever.
She weren't dangerous when they let her out;
so light, Buddy could lift her off the bed
with one arm and put her on the potty seat.
He made the potty seat out of some old rocker.
Buddy had a little patch out back; greens and peas.
Mable didn't have no teeth.
The first thing they do when you go crazy
is to pull the teeth.

Messages

Instead of grazing cattle,
this range is heavy with tires,
fenders, ball joints,
waiting for the good old boys
to come back, to steer
the good old cars;
Oldsmobiles, Studebakers, Pintos;
chrome flash.
Damn if they couldn't line the pockets
of old man Getty.
On a dark night, the stars,
the burnt out ones,
send their cinder dry messages
to these old cars.
Cheer up, they say, the Universe is ours.

Grade School

When I was nine and went to 82,
the winters were so cold.
I wore long stockings and laced up my shoes.
My teacher, Mrs. Ellery, was old;
very old. Her hair was black,
her teeth in back were gold.

Then when it snowed it was so deep and white;
it froze our stockings to our knees.
Mr. Vollar shoveled to the flag pole every night,
and every morning we'd hear his scrape and wheeze.

Mr. Vollar yodeled at recess.
He sat beside the furnace with his flute.
We laughed at everything he said in Swiss.
Even his laugh was guttural. He wore a green wool suit.
When he danced he clicked his heels.
Mrs. Ellery tapped the window panes.
Mr. Vollar's mustache dribbled yellow from his cheroot.

The building smelled like chalk.
Mr. Vollar dug long trenches to the door.
I carried my sandwich in a paper bag.
Our feet echoed on the wooden floor.
In that small room, that place apart,
sometimes Mr. Vollar fell asleep by the furnace.

Aesop, Shakespeare, Tennyson: at the start
of every day some poem we learned by heart.
Rose Lena Vollar, Mr. Vollar's daughter,
the shy giant of our class; her whispered
answers were correct and on lined paper,
her careful cursive loops were works of art.

Lines

Voice, perhaps you are the universe,
the hum of spiders.
If on the mountain a single bear
comes into the orchard;
much less, the husk of a locust
drops from the currant bush;
or the wind rattles a loose clapboard,
exchanging one skin for another –
it is the self longing to cross the barrier.
Sensing the visitors who hide among us,
the air enters and takes away.
Sharp as the odor of fresh sawdust,
the color of lost rooms,
those erotic odors, angst of brevity;
like crossing your thighs
in a spasm of loneliness.

On the Mountain

Drawing its thread,
the road
stretches
to where
it is not.
How forlorn;
and yet,
to stand still,
more so.
Or walking
the other way,
fear
rushes behind,
though it is only
the wind.

Tongues

To mortify the spirit I once attended
some classes of beginning French, et cetera.
And have I climbed toward heaven or descended?
It does not matter. I am not one
whom God can hope to save by dying twice.
I am lost among the words of sacrament.
What can I say but that I love the wind,
and I am shaken when it shakes and scatters
the stuttering leaves on the insensible pavement.

Half Sight in Middlebury

Now that I am almost blind in one eye,
I look at the blue up there
in this expanse of window, this
window in an apartment in mid-Vermont.
Sunday in mid-November, the white spires of the college,
sacred and quiet. The town's teenagers,
who haunt the early dark, are now asleep.
The couple who live under me are temporarily
appeased. The super and the manager
have let me know I must be more quiet when I get up
at two AM to pee. But that aside, here is the false holy
color of blue and I am inside the dome of this tennis ball
that something thwacked against the impossible.

This small middle-class town of buyers and sellers,
even here, drug-traffic and traffic drug.
The reckless egocentric driver and the shrewd pusher.
People of this town walk up and down,
looking for some filler for emptiness. To meet their standards
you must be mediocre middle-class mid-stream plastic.
You must speak their code from A to B and it helps to ski.

But this blue lifts over the old red brick and marble
stores butted together on either side of the street and divided
by the marble bridge that arches over the creek. Along one side
the library that threw out children's books like Selma Lagerlöf's
Nils and the Wonderful Goose since no one reads them anymore.

All dogs are leashed and you never see a cat; but birds,
sometimes in a small flock, sweep past my window;
their wings black against the deep deceptive blue.

Again I Find You

A compulsive flasher,
the limp kelp rises up
in the translucent wave;
like a drowned man,
arms reaching for help.
He crashes on the beach
and seethes, falling
slack, into himself.

Only the bird running down
to the foam edge;
running down and back
on its stilt legs,
from the dark stain
of the water's spread;
only the bird.

The Cabbage

You have rented an apartment.
You come to this enclosure with physical relief,
your heavy body climbing the stairs in the dark,
the hall bulb burned out, the landlord
of Greek extraction and possibly a fatalist.
In the apartment leaning against one wall,
your daughter's painting of a large frilled cabbage
against a dark sky with pinpoints of stars.
The eager vegetable, opening itself
as if to eat the air, or speak in cabbage
language of the meanings within meanings;
while the points of stars hide their massive
violence in the dark upper half of the painting.
You can live with this.

Three AM

You wake in the night. I know you do.
The first words: the café at the end of the street.
But the moon – the light has streaked the absurd silence,
the absurd silence of three AM
so that you begin to imagine snow,
the silence of snow adding to itself,
this place, this phenomenon
that approaches in pulses of strings.
Each rhythm of breath the listing of words, at the same time
the catacomb of windows across the way,
mysterious and utterly ordinary squares of light,
the drawn blinds; the surface of indifference.

To Try Again

"Tremble," says the sword-grass, leaning over the water.
"O, yes," the water-fractals sing, writhing in temporal ecstasy,
"Toward is inevitable. Fall to the center."
"Rushing, always rushing," sighs the larch, brushing the sky.
"Your roots are not deep enough. Try harder.
Apply yourself." On the milkweed, the larvae of the monarchs
grow against the pulsing heliosphere. "We must die
and be born again. The clouds of our endless selves
image the chrysalis. Yes, to become is the meaning."
"Look," says the void. "What meaning? Be thou me."

Not Expecting an Answer

This tedious letter to you…
what is one life to another?
We walk around inside our bags,
sucking it in, spewing it out.
Then the insects, swarms heavier
than all the animals of the world.
Then the flycatchers on the clothes line,
like seiners leaning from Flemish boats
when the seas were roiled with herring.
This long letter in my mind,
calligraphy, feathery asparagus.

Mantra

When I am sad
I sing, remembering
the redwing blackbird's clack.
Then I want no thing
except to turn time back
to what I had
before love made me sad.

When I forget to weep,
I hear the peeping tree toads
creeping up the bark.
Love lies asleep
and dreams that everything
is in its golden net;
and I am caught there, too,
when I forget.

About the Author

Ruth Stone won the 2002 National Book Award and the Wallace Stevens Award for *In the Next Galaxy*. Born in Virginia in 1915, she is the author of eight books of poetry, several chapbooks, and is the recipient of many honors, including a National Book Critics Circle Award, a Whiting Award, two Guggenheim Fellowships, the Delmore Schwartz Award, the Cerf Lifetime Achievement Award from the state of Vermont, the Bess Hokin Prize from *Poetry* magazine, and the Shelley Memorial Award. She raised three daughters alone while teaching creative writing at many universities, including the University of Illinois, University of Wisconsin, Indiana University, UC Davis, Brandeis, and finally settling at Binghamton University. She lives in Vermont.

Copper Canyon Press wishes to acknowledge the support of Lannan Foundation in funding the publication and distribution of exceptional literary works.

LANNAN LITERARY SELECTIONS 2002

Cesare Pavese, *Disaffections*, translated by Geoffrey Brock
Kenneth Rexroth, *The Complete Poems of Kenneth Rexroth*,
edited by Sam Hamill and Bradford Morrow
Alberto Ríos, *The Smallest Muscle in the Human Body*
Ruth Stone, *In the Next Galaxy*
C.D. Wright, *Steal Away: Selected and New Poems*

LANNAN LITERARY SELECTIONS 2001

Hayden Carruth, *Doctor Jazz*
Norman Dubie, *The Mercy Seat: Collected & New Poems, 1967–2001*
Theodore Roethke, *On Poetry & Craft*
Ann Stanford, Holding Our Own: *The Selected Poems of Ann Stanford*,
edited by Maxine Scates and David Trinidad
Reversible Monuments: Contemporary Mexican Poetry,
edited by Mónica de la Torre and Michael Wiegers

LANNAN LITERARY SELECTIONS 2000

John Balaban, Spring Essence: *The Poetry of Hồ Xuân Hương*
Sascha Feinstein, *Misterioso*
Jim Harrison, *The Shape of the Journey: New and Collected Poems*
Maxine Kumin, *Always Beginning: Essays on a Life in Poetry*
W.S. Merwin, *The First Four Books of Poems*

The Chinese character for poetry is made up of two parts: "word" and "temple." It also serves as pressmark for Copper Canyon Press. Founded in 1972, Copper Canyon Press remains dedicated to publishing poetry exclusively, from Nobel laureates to new and emerging authors. The Press thrives with the generous patronage of readers, writers, booksellers, librarians, teachers, students, and funders — everyone who shares the conviction that poetry invigorates the language and sharpens our appreciation of the world.

PUBLISHERS' CIRCLE

Allen Foundation for the Arts
Lannan Foundation
Lila Wallace-Reader's Digest Fund
National Endowment for the Arts

EDITORS' CIRCLE

Thatcher Bailey
Breneman Jaech Foundation
Cynthia Hartwig and Tom Booster
Port Townsend Paper Company
Target Stores
Emily Warn and Daj Oberg
Washington State Arts Commission

For information and catalogs:

COPPER CANYON PRESS
Post Office Box 271
Port Townsend, Washington 98368
360/385-4925
poetry@coppercanyonpress.org
www.coppercanyonpress.org

This book is set in Electra, created by American typographer and book designer W.A. Dwiggins in 1935. The book title is set in Nofret, created by calligrapher Gudrun Zapf von Hesse. Book design by Valerie Brewster, Scribe Typography.

9 781556 592072